In Fashion

Contents	Page
In fashion	2-3
In and out of fashion	4-5
Fads in fashion	6
One-off fashion	7
Mixed up fashion	8-9
Recycled fashion	10 - 11
At the land-fill site	12-13
Jeans	14-15
The way we dress	16

written by John Lockyer

Fashion is how we look. We can put on a top, some jeans, and a pair of shoes. If we go out and see people with the same clothes on, then we are in fashion.

What is fashion?

Pants that are in fashion can have rips, holes, roll-ups or cut-off legs. A T-shirt that is in fashion might be dull, very bright or just too big. The stuff we have can go out of fashion, too. It might be too big, too small, too tight, or too drab.

trends

fads in fashion

When a cap, handbag, shoes, or pants are in fashion, we see them everywhere. Many people want to be seen in them.

one-off

Some people do not like to wear these fads in fashion. They want to wear one-off items.

Some of us make our own fashion. We take items from hip hop, punk, goth, or geek fashion, and mix them up. This fashion can be fab but it can be a flop too.

recycled fashion

We can take old hats, shirts, tops, shoes, and jackets to a charity shop. These shops stop our stuff going to a land-fill site.

Items that are worn out can be recycled. They can be turned into rags, bags, shorts, and skirts.

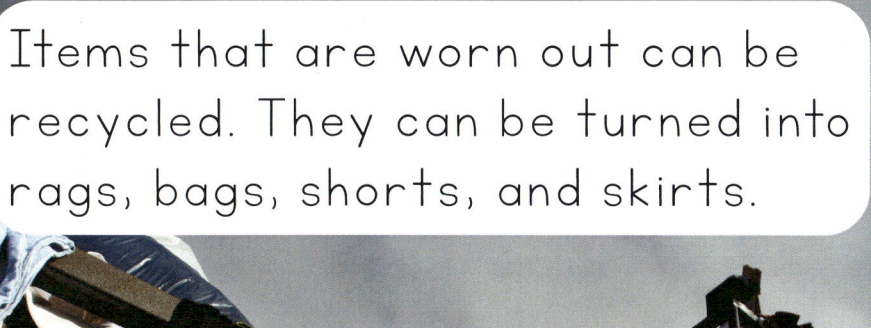

unwanted clothes

land-fill site

A lot of fashion items still end up as waste – but it takes a long time for them to rot.

We can stop this if we do not toss out stuff that is still good.

jeans

Jeans are an item that are in fashion all the time. We wear them at work and at home, too.

Take the zips, tags, and buttons off old jeans. Then you can turn them into a quilt, a bag, or a pet bed.

the way we dress

Items like a watch, a haircut, a belt, some sunglasses, a ring, and make-up are part of fashion, too.